**621.3986 Slater**
**Playing with Makey Makey**

# Playing with Makey Makey

## By Lindsay Slater

Published in the United States of America by
**Cherry Lake Publishing**
Ann Arbor, Michigan
www.cherrylakepublishing.com

Series Editor: Kristin Fontichiaro
Reading Adviser: Marla Conn, MD, Ed., Literacy Specialist,
Read-Ability, Inc.
Photo Credits: All photos by Lindsay Slater

Library of Congress Cataloging-in-Publication Data has been filed and is available
at catalog.loc.gov

Cherry Lake Publishing would like to acknowledge the work of the Partnership for
21st Century Learning. Please visit *www.p21.org* for more information.

Printed in the United States of America
Corporate Graphics

A Note to Adults: Please review the instructions for the activities in this book before allowing children to do them. Be sure to help them with any activities you do not think they can safely complete on their own.

A Note to Kids: Be sure to ask an adult for help with these activities when you need it. Always put your safety first!

# Table of Contents

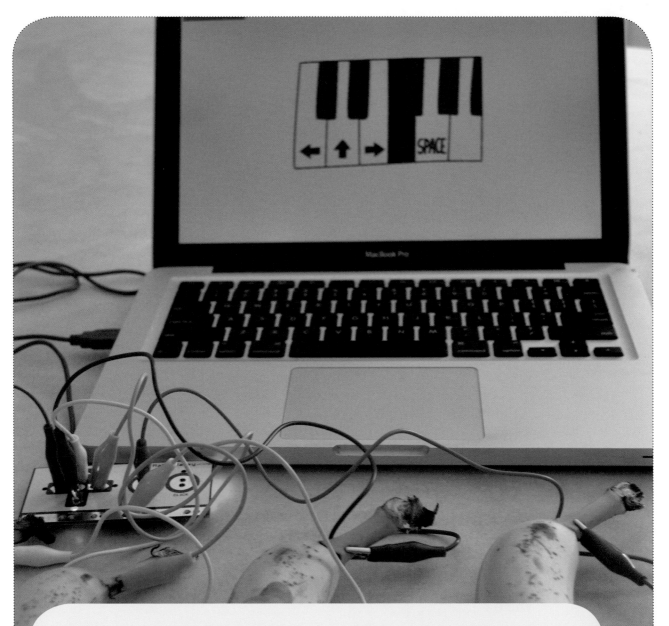

Have you ever played a banana piano? You can with Makey Makey Classic!

# What Is Makey Makey?

Many computers have keyboards. But have you ever seen a computer you can control with a banana? Makey Makey is a special tool. You can use it to invent new ways to talk to a computer. It works with bananas, play dough, and other cool things.

## Talking to Computers

When people invented the first computers, they did not use keyboards, mice, or touchscreens. They used paper cards to talk to computers. Sometimes they would need to use over a thousand cards at a time!

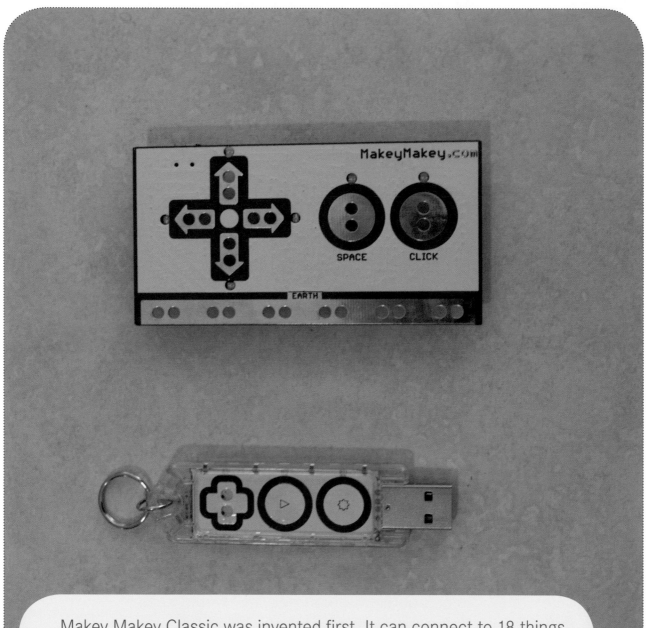

Makey Makey Classic was invented first. It can connect to 18 things at once. Makey Makey GO is smaller and newer. It can only connect to one thing at a time.

# Types of Makey Makeys

There are two kinds of Makey Makeys. They work in different ways. The first is called Makey Makey Classic. It uses **circuits**. It works if electricity can flow in a circle. The second kind is called Makey Makey GO. It senses the amount of electricity something can hold.

## Meet the Inventors

Makey Makey was created by Jay Silver and Eric Rosenbaum. They were students at the Massachusetts Institute of Technology. They wanted to create a tool for inventing things.

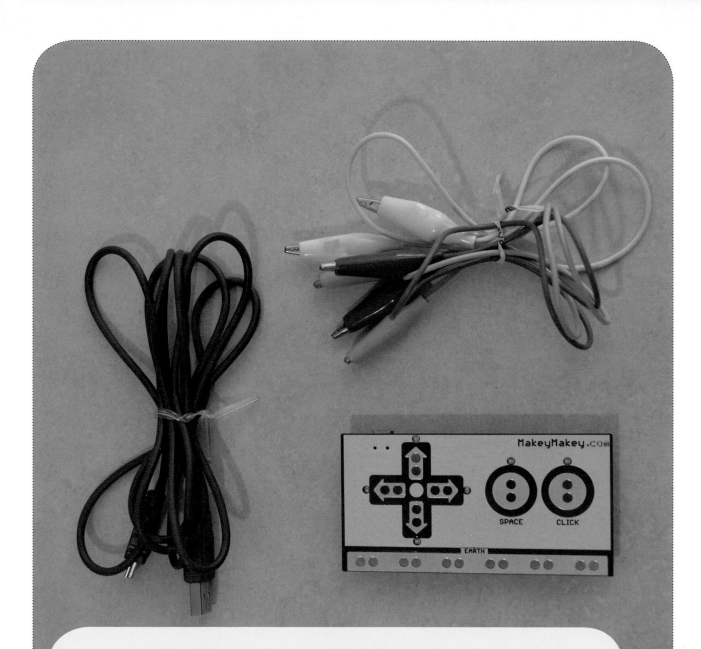

Makey Makey Classic comes with a cable. This is how it talks to the computer. The cable also powers the Makey Makey. Makey Makey Classic comes with alligator clips, too. You can use them to connect things to your Makey Makey.

# Makey Makey Classic Parts

Makey Makey Classic comes with a cable and wires with alligator clips. You can clip wires in several places on the Classic. Those places give the computer different messages, called **input**. Input from Makey Makey works just like when you click the mouse, press the space bar, or use arrow keys.

## What Does EARTH Do?

Look on your Makey Makey for the word EARTH. EARTH connects you to your Makey Makey. When you touch EARTH and another part of the Makey Makey, your body makes a circuit. This means electricity flows in a circle between the Makey Makey and you! It is only a small, safe amount of electricity.

We are completing a circuit between the left arrow and EARTH. When we open the drums program, we play a drum each time we touch the Makey Makey.

# Getting Started with Makey Makey Classic

1.  Plug one end of the cable into your Makey Makey. Plug the other end into the computer.
2.  Go to the following web page: *http://makeymakey.com/bongos*
3.  Attach an alligator clip to an EARTH space on your Makey Makey. Hold the other end of the cable in your hand.
4.  With your other hand, touch the left arrow on your Makey Makey. The computer should make a sound!

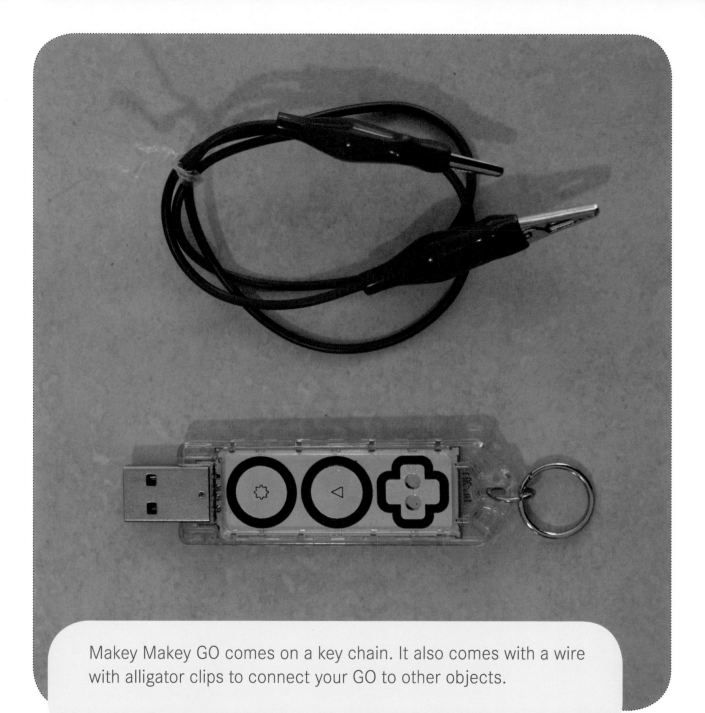

Makey Makey GO comes on a key chain. It also comes with a wire with alligator clips to connect your GO to other objects.

# Makey Makey GO Parts

Makey Makey GO is simpler. It plugs straight into the computer and uses just one alligator clip. It also has two special buttons. One is the Play button. The other is the Set button. You use the Set button to change your input. There are two options for input. If the light on the GO is blue, the Makey Makey tells the computer "mouse click." If the light is red, it tells the computer "space bar."

Makey Makey GO can also play the bongos program. The GO senses your body's electricity when you touch it.

# Getting Started with Makey Makey GO

1.  Plug Makey Makey GO into the computer.
2.  Go to the following web page: *http:// makeymakey.com/bongos*
3.  Tap the Play button.
4.  Now let's tell the Makey Makey which drum to play. Tap the Set button. Stop when the light is red. The red light means the input is set to "space bar."
5.  Tap the plus (+) shape. The computer should make a sound!

Here, we attached something metal to Makey Makey GO with the alligator clip. Now we can touch the penny instead of the GO. What happens if you connect a nickel instead? A dime? A quarter? Can you explain what is happening?

# Experimenting with Inputs

Makey Makey works if you tap it. It also works if you clip it to a penny and then touch the penny. This is because the penny **conducts** electricity through the wire to the Makey Makey. If you are using Makey Makey GO, press the Play button each time you clip it to a new object.

## What Can I Connect to Makey Makey?

You can connect anything that conducts electricity to your Makey Makey. Metals like pennies and aluminum foil conduct electricity. So do pencil lead and many vegetables!

Do you have play dough at home? It conducts electricity! Try using it to create a custom game controller!

# What Can I Do with Makey Makey?

You can use your Makey Makey instead of pressing a keyboard key or clicking a mouse. You can play games, take a picture, or make a sound. Some people have made their own Internet games and activities for Makey Makey. Ask an adult to help you find some online.

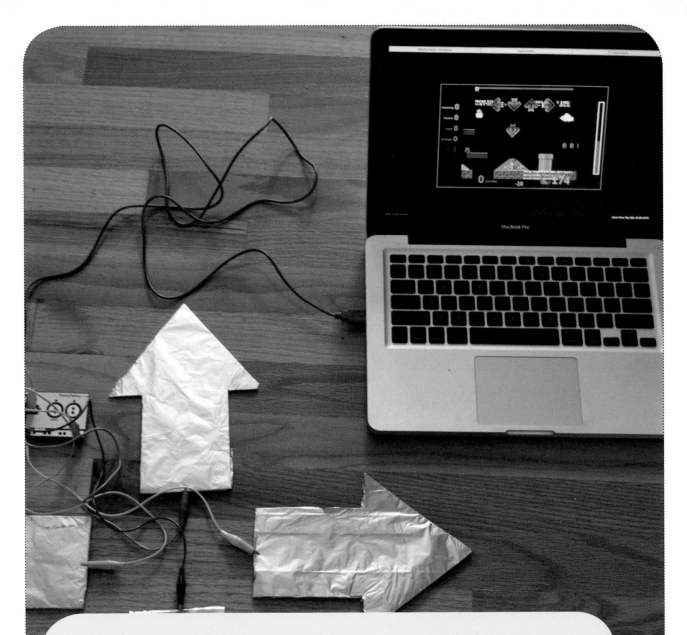

Aluminum foil conducts electricity. We cut arrows out of old cereal boxes and covered them with foil. When our bare foot touches the foil, we control the game.

# What If It Doesn't Work?

Sometimes your Makey Makey will not work. This happens to all inventors! Here are some things to try. Are you touching the alligator clip on the EARTH wire? Did you press the Play button on your GO? Maybe you need to change objects. Wood and plastic do not conduct electricity.

Keep trying! Soon you will learn what works best with your Makey Makey.

# Glossary

**circuits** (SUR-kits) uninterrupted paths along which electricity can flow

**conducts** (kuhn-DUKTS) allows electricity to pass through

**input** (IN-put) messages sent from a device to a computer

# Find Out More

**Books**

Matteson, Adrienne. *Coding with ScratchJr*. Ann Arbor, MI: Cherry Lake Publishing, 2017.

Ng, Sandy. *Makey Makey*. Ann Arbor, MI: Cherry Lake Publishing, 2016.

**Web Sites**

**Makey Makey**

*www.makeymakey.com*

Find examples of how to play with Makey Makey on the official website.

**Scratch**

*https://scratch.mit.edu*

On the Scratch website, you can play and make your own games. Many Scratch games can be played using Makey Makey.

# Index

## About the Author

Lindsay Slater likes reading, learning, and playing board games. She is a librarian for children and teens at a public library in Oregon.